T0145014

When Water Came FROM A Well

Anna Maria Garcia

WestBow Press books may be ordered through booksellers or by contacting:

WestBow Press
A Division of Thomas Nelson & Zondervan
1663 Liberty Drive
Bloomington, IN 47403
www.westbowpress.com
1 (866) 928-1240

ISBN: 978-1-9736-4185-8 (sc)
ISBN: 978-1-9736-4186-5 (e)

Library of Congress Control Number: 2018911803

Print information available on the last page.

WestBow Press rev. date: 10/4/2018

WESTBOW
PRESS®
A DIVISION OF THOMAS NELSON
& ZONDERVAN

When Water Came FROM A Well

When houses still had dirt floors, women brought water in buckets from the well, and families spent time baking sweet treats passed down from generation to generation, my daddy came to town from "El Norte".

He came loaded with boxes full of goodies for the men and women. He brought bed sheets sets, t-shirts, ball point pens, and towels. Beach towels, pastel colored towels, hand and bath towels. But he mostly brought umbrellas. Brightly colored umbrellas for the women who did a lot of walking back and forth carrying water from the well. Walking under the scorching sun.

When my daddy came to town everyone got a fluffy towel or an umbrella. Later, he would sit under a mesquite tree and wait for the paleta man to arrive.

The paleta man hadn't arrived to the mesquite tree, and already he was trailed by all the children in town as he dinged his hand bell. Little children, big children, naked children and happy children came to see my dad under the mesquite tree.

The cart full of paletas would stop under that mesquite tree and my daddy would buy every Popsicle from that cart.

All the children went back to their houses either licking a Popsicle or just a piece of ice, but with a dollar in their pockets for the next time.

The Popsicle man rested under that mesquite tree because his work was all done.

Daddy did the same thing with the baker. . .

The fruit man. . .

He had plenty of money because, after all, he had money from "El Norte". That's when the dollar was worth something, people were hungry, and grateful.

In small towns years pass very slowly, but they are not immune from the passage of time. All of sudden, one day everybody had dirt floors covered with pretty tile and concrete, water come pouring from a faucet, and children lost interest in Popsicles, sweets without a recipe, or fruit in a cup. Women had no need for umbrellas. People were only interested in color television and the goods it promoted.

My daddy stopped taking his boxes full of umbrellas and towels and sheets to El rancho.

Instead, he took Viva and blue industrial napkins to the mechanic in the city who was having a hard time making his business take off. He took disposable plates to a single mother who was selling tacos from five in the morning to 10 at night. He loaded his truck with wood for the young man who was starting a new family. And plenty of shoes. Leather shoes, soft shoes, steel-toe shoes, grown up shoes and baby shoes.

He loaded plenty of boxes. Boxes and chairs. Wheelchairs, highchairs, and rocking chairs. Later, I asked him, "Why, daddy? Why do you take all that stuff?" He said, "Because I remember. I don't have to stop and become like others. I remember."

He continued taking his boxes 2,000 miles one way for over 50 years. Boxes full of shoes, paper products, clothes, or whatever was needed. He risked his life and health even though he didn't have a single relative in Mexico anymore.

One day he said, "It is your responsibility to go and see where you are needed."

Printed in the United States
By Bookmasters